MW00512491

NFT: TOP MARKETPLACES

How to Buy and Invest: Success Stories.
Nft & Real Estate Disruptive Projects.

James Parker

© Copyright 2018 by James Parker. All rights reserved.

This document is geared towards providing exact and reliable information regarding topic and issue covered. The publication is sold with the idea that the publisher is not required to render accounting, officially permitted, or otherwise, qualified services. If advice is necessary, legal or professional, a practiced individual in the profession should be ordered.

From a Declaration of Principles which was accepted and approved equally by a Committee of the American Bar Association and a Committee of Publishers and Associations.

In no way is it legal to reproduce, duplicate, or transmit any part of this document in either electronic means or in printed format. Recording of this publication is strictly prohibited and any storage of this document is not allowed unless with written permission from the publisher. All rights reserved.

The information provided herein is stated to be truthful and consistent, in that any liability, in terms of inattention or otherwise, by any usage or abuse of any policies, processes, or directions contained within is the solitary and utter responsibility of the recipient reader. Under no circumstances will any legal responsibility or blame be held against the publisher for any reparation, damages, or monetary loss due to the information herein, either directly or indirectly. Respective authors own all copyrights not held by the publisher.

The information herein is offered for informational purposes solely, and is universal as so. The presentation of the information is without contract or any type of guarantee assurance.

The trademarks that are used are without any consent, and the publication of the trademark is without permission or backing by the trademark owner. All trademarks and brands within this book are for clarifying purposes only and are the owned by the owners themselves, not affiliated with this document.

Sommario

TOP MARKETPLACES

Each marketplace has its own philosophy, and new ones pop up all the time. That's why you need to discover them, learn about them, and choose the best one for your art and your style before opening your own gallery. The platform can also make a difference in establishing the value and popularity of your works.

ASYNC ART (HTTPS://ASYNC.ART/)

Async Art is a recent art movement built on the blockchain.

Within it, you can create, collect, and exchange programmable art. This is art that can evolve over time, respond to a stimulus, trigger a reaction from its owners, or follow an exchange price. You can purchase both "Masters" and "Layers." A Master is a 1/1 edition artwork, while Layers are the individual components that make up the Master image.

Layers come with special abilities chosen by the artist. When you edit something on a layer, the aster image will reflect it regardless of who owns it. Artists pick the parameters of their art and grant exclusive control over each aspect to individual collectors. For example, they might enable someone to modify the state of the background, the color of the sky, or the position of a character.

FOUNDATION (HTTPS://FOUNDATION.APP/)

The particularity of this marketplace is that it is curated by the community. In practice, the creators selected only the first 50 artists, who then extended invitations to others and created the community. Invitations are limited for now. To become part of the community, it is advisable to make friends with members from whom you can then request an invitation—perhaps starting conversations with artists or collectors with common interests or whose work you admire. Sharing their work on social media could be a great way to make friends and build a relationship. On February 19, 2021, the famous gif of the Nyan Cat sold at a Foundation platform auction for $545 thousand in Ether. KNOWNORIGIN HTTPS://KNOWNORIGIN.IO/

To become part of the gallery of Knownorigin, it is

also essential to be selected. The process of selection ensures that the works are of an acceptable quality and follow the philosophy behind the platform. Most of the marketplaces present themselves through Medium, through which they share their philosophy and manage a blog section dedicated to the major works in their gallery. Each digital artwork on KnownOrigin is authentic and truly unique. The Ethereum blockchain protects it.

MAKERSPLACE HTTPS://MAKERSPLACE.COM/

MakersPlace has been an active crypto art market since 2018 and is based in the United States. It is considered a high-value gallery.

The long list of creators with NFT sold on this market include names like Yura Miron, Silvio Veira, Dmitri Cherniak, Dreamonaut, and Frenetik Void, to name a few.

MakersPlace's primary focus is exclusive digital art, but it also features some less exclusive art. NFTs are based on the ETH blockchain. To gain access, you have to apply and be selected.

On MakersPlace, you have to pay a 15% service fee. We are not aware of any other NFT marketplaces that charge a higher commission than this, but a few charge exactly this (15%). There are also 12.50% commissions for any secondary sales on MakersPlace, of which 2.50% goes to MakersPlace, and 10% goes to the creator as a royalty. These fees are separate from the Ethereum gas fees that the Ethereum network requires to process transactions.

Every digital creation on MakersPlace is digitally signed by the creator and permanently recorded and verified through the blockchain. MakersPlace provides and manages a unique digital wallet for each creator.

MINTABLE (HTTPS://MINTABLE.APP/)

Mintable allows you to create NFTs totally free of charge by ensuring that the gas cost is paid at the time of the first sale. Mintable is a cutting-edge platform in which Mark Cuban has invested and which has auctioned the work of the 20th-century Ukrainian artist Wladimir Baranoff-Rossiné, whose works are managed by his descendants. The auction included an abstract painting from 1925 that had remained in the family since its creation and that was linked directly to an NFT on Mintable. In addition, nine digital representations of other Baranoff-Rossiné paintings, the originals of which the family will obviously retain ownership of, will also be sold with NFTs in three limited-edition auctions. This is a physical work certified on the blockchain by the platform itself. On Mintable, it is possibleto buy and sell not only on the Ether circuit but also in Zilliqa with ZIL.

NIFTY GATEWAY (HTTPS://NIFTYGATEWAY.COM/)

Since 2019, Nifty Gateway has been owned by the Gemini Exchange company, founded by the Winklevoss twins, who are most known for their lawsuit against Mark Zuckerberg in which they claimed Facebookownership. The platform's mission is to make the world of NFT accessible to everyone. On Nifty Gateway, you can buy, sell, exchange, and show so- called "Nifties" (name the platform gives NFTs). There are also various collaborations among the platform and the best artists worldwide, among which the famous American painter Micheal Kagan, one of the first traditional artists to approach the world of crypto art, stands out. To sell your works, you need to fill out an application, make a presentation, and wait for the selection process. Once accepted, each uploaded collection will be open at a specific time (a drop) and will only be available for a limited time. New drops are expected approximately once every three weeks. After a collection's initial drop closes or runs out, you'll only be able to get Nifties from that collection in the marketplace. On Nifty Gateway, each time an artwork is purchased and sold, the artist gets a percentage of the sales. The artist can also decide on their own rate for secondary sales, which could be 5% 50%. Nifty Gateway takes 5% + 30 cents on each secondary sale to cover credit card processing fees and as an expense of running the platform.

OPENSEA (HTTPS://OPENSEA.IO/)

Founded in 2017, OpenSea supports NFT with ERC721 and ERC1155 standards. It is the largest NFT marketplace, containing over 200 categories and millions of assets. It provides a wide range of NFTs, including art, censorship-resistant domain names, virtual worlds, figurines, sports, and collectibles.

It, too, is open to anyone who wants to join, and

you can add NFTs from different marketplaces. It has a rich blog section with the latest news and guides to create and sell independently, but the most inspiring part is the activities section, where you can keep an eye on all the latest offers and trends.

PORTION (HTTPS://PORTION.IO/)

Portion is an online marketplace that connects artists and collectors through blockchain technology to buy, sell, and invest in art and collectibles easily with total transparency. It includes the Artist Community, a global network of decentralized creators and artists. Here, anyone can be a collector.

You can control your physical and digital collection in one place, simplifying cryptocurrency exchange with art and collectibles. Portion tokens are ERC-20 resources on the Ethereum Blockchain, and members can govern and vote on the platform's future in a decentralized way.

RARIBLE (HTTPS://RARIBLE.COM/)

Rarible is a platform that is suitable for everyone,

even beginners, and it's open, which means that you don't need to be selected to start creating NFTs on Rarible. Secondary sales take place on Rarible's marketplace; there are royalty options, and both single items and entire collections can be sold in bundles.

Rarible is a community-owned NFT marketplace. Its "owners" hold the RARI ERC-20 token. Rarible awards the RARI token to active users on the platform who buy or sell on the NFT marketplace. Creators can use Rarible to "mint" new NFTs to sell their artworks, including books, music albums, digital art, or movies. Creators can also show a preview of their creation butlimit the entire project to the buyer only. Rarible buys and sells NFTs in categories such as art, photography, games, metaverse, music, domains, memes, and more.

SUPERRARE HTTPS://SUPERRARE.CO/

As with other marketplaces, to have a collection on SuperRare, you must go through a selection process. SuperRare focuses on being a marketplace where people buy and sell unique, single edition digital artwork. The team has to make sure that the works are original, created by real artists, and, most importantly, unique. On SuperRare, as anticipated, you can only sell single pieces and not series, and buyers have free access to the platform through MetaMask. Here, you can only use Ethereum for payments. The platform retains 15% of sales on the primary market and 10% on thesecondary market for artists. SuperRare has also been chosen as a platform by *Time* Magazine, the famous American publication, which has auctioned three digital covers with the help of renowned entrepreneur, investor, and influencer Anthony Pompliano.

THE MINT FUND (HTTPS://MINT.AF/)

Networks like The Mint Fund, which cover the fees needed for artists to mint their first tokens, suggest that real-life social ties are being built thatare far stronger than the blockchain. Mint Fund is a community project created with the sole purpose of building a support network for artistsinterested in bringing their art to the world of cryptocurrencies like NFT. The project aims to offer resources to foster a diverse community by allowing artists to coin their work simply by filling out a form. Art has the unique ability to highlight inequalities globally and shine a spotlight on ongoing social movements. That's why initiatives like The Mint Fund are born and remain essential to the development of sustainable and inclusive art.

HOW TO BUY AND INVEST

Buying crypto art is practically and technically quite simple. Once you understand how cryptocurrency and wallet work, what's left to do is choose. And for a collector or investor, this is a crucial step. Once you have purchased the desired amount of ETH through platformslike Coinbase, you need to connect your wallet to the platform where you want to shop.

Most marketplaces have an activity section that allows you to check the ranking of artists, and thus, choose the one that suits your tastes and what you want to spend. Besides, you can keep an eye on the artists who sell the most and on what kind of prices their artwork goes for. If you spot an inspiring artist, you can view their page and works, and then filter and sort the pieces from the lowest to the highest price. Otherwise, on the main page, you can browse all the creations within a price range that don'tnecessarily belong to a single artist. Once you have identified the piece you want to buy, you can either purchase it right away or make an offer for the amount you are willing to spend and let the artist decide whether to accept your proposition or not. The purchased piece appears in the wallet in about 10 minutes, following the creation of the transaction on the blockchain.

Getting started with collecting is quick and easy as well. No middleman is required. If you make an offer to an artist and they decide to accept it, the piece will be awarded to you. This process is fast, usually immediate, transparent, and secure. Once you have acquired digital ownership of the work, anyone can take the entire collection with them at any time. You can then give it away to whomever you wish across the planet, and storing the digitally encrypted work becomes much more straightforward than owninga traditional piece. Both primary and secondary sales are fully observable and transparent, but also completely anonymous if you wish. In the digital world, one challenge that is still considered impossible to overcome concerns the authenticity of one's work. However, today's platforms that sell crypto art in the form of non-fungible tokens have incorporated selling by selection. Selection allows for stronger input controls that will enable marketplaces to check that the artwork is authentic without preventinganyone from selling their art.

MAKE PROFIT

In the past, auction houses, billionaires, private collectors, and investors from around the world set the prices and values of works in the marketplace; these same interests will keep the NFT marketplace alive, active, and profitable for a very long time. Cryptographic digital artwork has immense capabilities, and it is inevitably taking over the world.

At present, solutions for issues regarding preservation, liability, and insurance are gradually being found. As new instances emerge, improvements are being created. This living market does not stop; it improves over time, intending to gain more and more respect, credibility, and recognition, especially with the general public.

Soon, collecting digital art will become standard practice. Moreover, while traditional galleries risk being left behind, there is a golden opportunity to invest in an emerging, secure, young, and dynamic market that generates value at an exponential rate. The timing is optimal for investing: tokenized art is cutting edge, accessible, and in step with the digital times.

Investing at this time is profitable for several reasons:

• It is the token itself that generates value. By creating scarcity for a work that is potentially accessible to all, it is the artwork itself that produces value for its buyer through circulation.

• Total NFT sales during a single month in 2020 were $250,000. Today, in the same month, the total reached $60 million, and the trend continues to move upward.

Profits will be huge and will increase because NFTs are not a temporary trend but a new way for modern generations to understand, conceive of, and collect art. Knowing the artists and following them on social networks allows everyone to verify their identity and achieve popularity. It is possible to choose the artists you are most interested in based on personal parameters or opt for those who break the rules and redefine a canon or those who have something to say and a story to tell.

If you still have doubts about investing in crypto art, just consider that the art market has always been resilient and has proven that it is able to renew itself and resist any collapse. Starting to collect today means being able to become, perhaps, a patron of the future or invest wisely to reach a higher level of liquidity in the not-too-distant future, given the speed at which new technological innovations travel.

LIMITING RISKS

It is not possible to know a world in depth without relating it to its potential risks.

One NFT risk is price fluctuation due to the number of people using the blockchain network. Each time you tokenize an artwork, you are creating a new block to add to the chain. To do this, a computing power is used that is expressed through a gas cost. More transactions simultaneously increase theprice of this fee, and then the creation and sale of the work increase their value. The fluctuation of the value on Ethereum should also be taken into consideration.

Not all artists can afford to pay a high gas fee, which prevents them from expressing their art. In addition, platforms retain a commission on their sales, although this is not much of a real risk since platforms still charge a smaller commission than a regular art gallery.

A single Ethereum transaction requires the energy to power a computational network that eventually creates a new NFT and generates a considerable amount of CO2. A frequently cited statistic from Ethereum's Energy Consumption Index pegs the average transaction at nearly 60-kilowatt hoursor two days' worth of energy for an average North American household. This factor also contributes to the decrease in minted artwork, at least as far as artists who care about the environment are concerned.NFTs took hold immediately, quickly, and competitively. On the one hand, they have allowed the sudden renewal of contemporary art, improving the outlook for digital art. On the other hand, they have attracted many reflections about critical issues that still need to be fully resolved. Thus far, the consolidated market is not particularly clear, so it is not easy to understand how to become a professional artist or collector of NFT. The crypto art market needs internal regulations to be developed in the meantime as this world continues to grow. But the growth is inordinate and fast enough to raise doubts and questions.

Beeple, who now collaborates regularly with Christie's, is building zero- emission routes by investing part of his revenue in renewable energy. Artists and marketplaces are the ones who will be able to change thedirection and reduce the impact of emissions on Ethereum. One optimal solution is to replace the Proof of Work validation system with Ethereum 2.0's Proof of Stake, in which the systems chosen for the computational effort are chosen randomly and in fewer numbers. This could reduce the CO_2 emissions caused by the blockchain by up to 99%.

New projects are being created all the time that start from the bottom, such as Fractional, which allows NFT owners to issue fractional ownership of their works. Fractional allows owners to collect some of the cash associatedwith their asset without selling the work. It is a decentralized protocol that enables artists and investors to understand the marketability of the product. For example, selling a fractional piece at a price helps you understand how the market values that piece overall.

Fractional works through NFT vault, a sort of repository, which takes on therole of the custodian of the property and allows it to be fractional, after which the artist can auction, give away, or sell their fractional token. In this way, the ERC721 is transformed into an ERC20, then into a fungible token that can be traded and generate liquidity. Fractional artwork solves the liquidity problem of NFTs. This type of innovation is experimental and encourages the entry of implementations that are essential to ensure that risks are limited and the entire process is facilitated and secure.

SUCCESS STORIES

Morons (White), or Bansky the Provocateur

An incredible case of success for investors was Bansky's entry into the NFT market. The artist known to the world for his provocative verve has been at the center of a real market operation of incredible value. One of his creations, "Morons" (White), was sold by the Taglialatela gallery of New York to the decentralized blockchain company Injective Protocol for
$96,000.

With a careful marketing campaign, the company tokenized the work on OpenSea and then burned the physical canvas by posting a live video on the Burnt Bansky Twitter account. In this way, the only original work with all of the same specifications and, therefore, recognized as an authentic Bansky drawing became the one on the blockchain. Injective Protocol could sell it for four times their original purchase price. This is a truly incredible marketing success that generated a lot public buzz.

WarNymph: Visual Art and Music at the Service of Success

The Canadian singer Grimes, also known for being the companion of Elon Musk, one of the richest men in the world, entered the world of NFT with a project called WarNymph Collection 1, which sold for $5.8 million and is already considered one of the most desired collectibles in the world.

Together with her brother, the artist combined visual concepts with tattooed cherubs and angels along with pieces of her original music and sold all 10 of her NFT works in less than 20 minutes on Nifty Gateway.

Very appropriately, some of the NFT reproductions featured cherubs and angels protecting Mars, the planet that Elon Musk intends to reach within a few years with SpaceX.

Those who bought these works did so with the prospect of seeing their value increase exponentially. WarNymph is Grimes's virtual avatar and has been used to promote her new album, and WarNymph Collection 1 is part of this fantastic promotional campaign. Thus, as soon as the album drops, those who bought the tokens will find themselves with an even more desirable object.

And, if SpaceX reaches its goal, the value can be expected to soar. It is an exciting short- or long-term investment.

Homer Pepe: Art According to Generation Z

To understand the investment value of this work of art that sold for
$320,000, you have to start far from the character of Pepe the Frog, which was created by artist Matt Furie and inspired several memes, including Rare Pepe.

In the wake of these highly successful memes, Joe Looney generated the card Homer Pepe, a collector's item that includes Homer Simpson in the guise of Pepe the Frog. This NFT was purchased for a price of $38,500. However, the seriality of the meme and its recognizability enabled it to acquire a significantly higher value. When the owner, Peter Kell, decided tosell, he did so at almost ten times its original purchase value.

Nyan the Cat: Virality as an Added Value

Also known as Pop Tart Cat, this work of art represents typical modern digital art, and its immediate virality showed the power of the Internet to share and transform different works.

According to creator Chris Torres, "Originally, its name was Pop Tart Cat, and I will continue to call it so, but the Internet has reached a decision to name it Nyan Cat, and I'm happy with that choice, too."

The value granted by the GIF's recognition and virality enabled the NFT to be sold for a sum equal to half a million dollars.

Bitcoin Angel or a $3 Million Mash-up

Trevor Jones combined his inspiration with the iconic sculpture of Gian Lorenzo Bernini in this NFT, and, in less than 7 minutes, he managed to achieve one of the largest sales in the history of non-fungible tokens.

By selling 4,157 versions of the Bitcoin Angel work at $777 each, theauthor made $3.2 million. Collectors who decided to buy a version of the work now own an original that is worth much more than the original sale price if only for the fame it has acquired.

Everydays - The First 5000 Days: The Most Expensive NFT in History

The American artist Beeple, in collaboration with Christie's auction house,

generated a total of $69 million for his work. The proceeds made him the third most expensive living artist in the world, increase the value of all his other works, and ensured his place in the Olympus of crypto artists.

The race to buy was tight, with Justin Sun, a digital entrepreneur, narrowly missing out on winning; his $70 million counteroffer, in fact, occurred asthe auction was closing.

Beeple shows how the most enterprising collectors and the most famous auction houses are investing heavily in NFTs. Moreover, it reveals how, justa few years after their birth, these works of art have developed into a flourishing and creative market of extreme importance.

Jack Dorsey, Twitter, and Non-fungible Tokens

Jack Dorsey, the genius and billionaire inventor of Twitter, sold his first tweet for almost $3 million. As a demonstration of the interest of the marketfor

NFTs, a Malaysian entrepreneur, Sina Estavi, CEO of Bridge Oracle, made the purchase and found himself the owner of the first message ever launched on one of the most famous social networks in the world. Some have compared this sale to having purchased a famous autograph.

Jack Dorsey's bet also ends with an even better happy ending, as the entire sum of the sale was donated to charity.

José Delbo, the Masked Superhero

José Delbo, born in 1933, is one of the most renowned comic book artists inthe world, owner of some of the most famous drawings, and sought after bycollectors of comics. Thus, when he entered the NFT market with crypto artist Trevor Jones, the web went crazy.

An oil version of one of the inked drawings of the dark knight, Batman, has been tokenized and put up for sale on MakersPlace for $552,603.98. The lucky investor will own not only an extraordinary collectible NFT but also the first official digital DC Comics artwork. This means that he will be the absolute owner of the work that marks the entrance of DC Comics into the world of crypto art, a record that will add even more value to this investment over time.

The New York Times Sells an Article: Art and Literature come Together

The article titled "Buy this Column on Blockchain" was written by journalist Kevin Roose. The article was sold on Foundation for $563,000, but it had been published in paper and on the web just the day before. The buyer became the owner of a piece of history that will never fade away: the first article ever to be sold as an NFT. In addition, the money was donated to the Neediest Cases Fund.

BEST INNOVATIVE ARTISTS AND THEIR PROJECTS

Beeple https://www.beeple-crap.com/

American Mike Winkelmann is better known as Beeple, a name so famous that it has become practically synonymous with success. His story is one of passion and a long apprenticeship. In 2007, Beeple decided that he wouldn't let a day go by without creating a work of art.

He started by drawing his Uncle Jim. Five thousand days later, the equivalent of over 13 and a half years, he became the creator of the third highest priced work of art sold while alive in the entire history of art, behind only Jeff Koons' Rabbit and Portrait of an Artist (Pool with Two Figures).

Everydays: The First 5000 Days is the name of the work in question. It is a collage of 21,069 x 21,069 pixels containing all the works Beeple created in those first 5000 days. Thus, there is a well-defined story behind the birth of this extraordinary artist who has been able to effectively represent himself and his dedication to his craft.

Blake Kathryn
https://twitter.com/blakekathryn

Blake Kathryn is a visual artist from Los Angeles who works with the most important chains in the world from Adidas, Adobe, Fendi, and Facebook to Warner Bros, Columbia Records, and many others. Her artistic conceptionis so atypical and particular that she has been included among the most interesting and influential artists in the NFT field.

Her Venuses, women queens who rule the winds and seasons, have been sold on Nifty Gateway for over $1,500 each. The famous entrepreneur and heiress Paris Hilton, in collaboration with Blake, has launched "PlanetParis," her first collection of NFT composed of three pieces already sold outon the Nifty Gateway platform.

Chris Torres https://twitter.com/prguitarman

If you associate the term meme economy with NFT, you can't help but thinkof Chris Torres, the creator of the gif "Nyan the Cat," a meme that sold for over $600,000. This crypto artist from Dallas, Texas created the gif in 2011,and it immediately exploded in a proliferation of shares and popularity. "Nyan the Cat" is, in fact, a network phenomenon of global proportions. PRguitarman, Chris's pseudonym, is the most shining example of a new reality that advances a unique concept of digital art that eradicates old concepts in favor of a fluid, digital, and hyperconnected world.

Dotpigeon https://www.dotpigeon.com/

Dotpigeon, a 33-yea-old from Milan, is notorious among crypto artists. When his works were auctioned on Nifty Gateway, they sold out almost instantly and earned him over 1 million euros.

His is an excellent story of victory. He worked for a web-based advertising agency while trying to break through as a digital artist. Now, his art is recognized globally, and he has decided to devote himself exclusively to that.

This artist, who wears a black balaclava as a rebellion against the social masks of bourgeois capitalism, is fascinating because he has been able to combine his skill as an artist with brilliant personal promotion. In fact, he talked about himself on Discord, presented at the Milan Plan X Art Gallery, and proposed that he be added to the Instagram page Larry's List, which reports the most interesting artists of the moment.

Giovanni Motta https://giovannimotta.it/

The Italian Giovanni Motta also represents the vanguard in the new and avant-garde world of crypto art. Born in Verona, this 50-year-old combines past and future in his works; his favorite protagonist is, Jonny Boy, the representation of his childhood self-inserted into the digital world of NFT art.

After devoting a lifetime to perfecting his art,

Giovanni Motta is one of the most well-known artists on SuperRare. He is recognized as one of the best-known names in crypto art, and his drawings, which are inspired in part by oriental culture and manga, explore the inner world of adults as they try to retain that fundamental part of their ego linked to childhood.

Hackatao https://podmork.com/blogmork/

Starting from solid experience with neo-pop and pop surrealism in theItalian market of tangible art, they were the first to tokenize art on SuperRare. The artistic minds behind the project are Sergio Scalet and Nadia Squarci. The real pioneers of crypto art in Italy and around the world, they are part of the beating heart of the digital exchange. They started by proposing an engaging and stimulating experience for traditional collectors and directing them toward the crypto art market. Compared to conventional media, with crypto art, they have experimented with a faster means of expression. Hackatao denounces the contemporary world's contradictions, and their art has an optimistic outlook that is wide open to the digital future in which they claim the right to express themselves without censorship or false idols.

Josh Pierce https://www.joshpierce.net/

Josh Pierce is a digital artist famous for his 3D NFTs. With over 100,000 followers on Instagram, he has become a protagonist on the world scene since his first appearance on Nifty Gateway. He defines himself as a visual artist and a motion graphics art director, and he focuses on themes that combine surrealism and naturalism, trying to create awe and spiritual calm by expressing the presence of spirituality in every present moment. His skillis the result of a long apprenticeship. In addition to being an NFT artist, he has also collaborated with the NFLLeague of American Football, Adobe, and multiple Grammy-winning artists.

Kevin Abosh https://www.kevinabosch.com/

The visionary Irish artist Kevin Abosh is linked to the IAMA Coins project and is one of the most inspiring and controversial digital artists. His turning point toward crypto art happened in 2016, when he sold a work of art that represented a potato for 1 million euros and was overwhelmed by thefeeling that he had commodified himself. As a result, he decided to rebel against this by literally selling himself.

The IAMA Coins project binds 10,000,000 NFT works connected to 100 physical works by alphanumeric codes. The peculiarity of the whole thing is that these real works were made from his own blood. He literally tokenized and sold himself.

Incredibly active and always attentive to the current moment, he has created collaborations with other artists, inspired industry hashtags, and much more.

Pak https://twitter.com/muratpak

An example of personal storytelling, Pak is one of the most famous and well-known digital artists globally, earning the nickname of omniscient designer/developer/magician despite maintaining complete anonymity. Indeed, no one even knows if Pak is a single artist or a collective. Pak's identity is shrouded in mystery. What is known is that Pak is the founder and lead designer of the Undream studio and the creator of Archillect, an artificial intelligence built to discover and share stimulating visual content on different social media. Archillect is a real digital revolution because it is configured as a digital curator that, thanks to specific keywords, can search for images with minimal and aesthetically cold tones, in complete autonomy, without requiring external human mediation.

The auction house Sotheby's has chosen to collaborate with Pak for its entry into the digital world.

Pak is certainly not a newcomer, having been present in the digital art world for over 20 years, and is a compelling demonstration of how one must learn not only to tell their story in an original way but also be patient about developing their craft for the right amount of time before garnering attention. Pak's admirers include Elon Musk, the CEO of Tesla and SpaceX.

Trevor Jones

https://www.trevorjonesart.c

om/nfts.html

Trevor Jones is a Scottish artist who can claim a prominent place among

digital artists who have linked their works to the blockchain. He creates digital drawings inspired by the great works of past artists and then animates them. His Picasso's Bull sold for $55,555.55, the largest Nifty Gateway sale since the platform's inception.

The artist is so famous that DC Comics chose him to work together with comic artist José Delbo and lead the publishing house's entrance into the world of NFTs with crypto art dedicated to Batman.

Xcopy

https://xcopyart.com/portfolio/tagged/nft

Digital artist and cryptocurrency enthusiast based in London, Xcopy's distinctive and fascinating collections can be found on SuperRare and on Nifty Gateway. He maintains close ties with the entire community interested in   NFTs, often delivering positivity and personal   growth   messages. Xcopy has become a true mentor to many.

His digital art investigates dystopia, death, and apathy through distortedimages reproduced in a loop and has achieved extraordinary success.

NFT AND REAL ESTATE

There is nothing more real in today's world than technology, and NFTsare proving it in a disruptive way. A universe no longer a nichewhose sales have exceeded 250 million dollars and continue to grow day by day.

Collecting, selling but above all, investing and earning are the key words behind NFT. The capital is increasing more and more, and so is the interest in these products. How does an intangible asset that everyone can seeachieve such value? How and who can create and sell their works in NFTs?

What applications and results can they generate in the future? Is this astable market in which to invest? Selling, collecting, investing, and earning, these and many others, are the possibilities that make non-fungible tokens a real technological bubble that is interesting and appealing to many. An interest that will not be extinguished and will find more and more market and uses. So many famous names have helped make NFTs even more popular. Non-fungible tokens are a unique resource of their kind. And in fact, everything about the interest and value of non-fungible tokens refers to uniqueness. What the non-fungible token creates is verifiable digital scarcity.

NFTs can be a revolution in terms of the many possibilities.

NFTS AND APPLICATION AREAS

Since Mike Winkelmann, aka Beeple, sold his digital work for just under $70 million, NFTs have become popular with the general public. More precisely, on March 11, 2021, at 4 p.m., what can now be called a true NFT mania exploded. NFT stands for Non-Fungible Token, which is a digital information recorded on the blockchain. These tokens are called non- fungible precisely because they are not interchangeable; they are unique and cannot be divided. What is special about NFTs is precisely their uniqueness and non-replicability, which makes non-fungible tokens so appealing. These tokens are cryptographic, meaning they represent something unique, such as a work of art, music, or any other collectible, and digitally certify ownership. Before NFTs, it was nearly impossible to authenticate and own a digital asset.

Although it is a phenomenon that exploded recently, it is impossible to say that non-fungible-tokens have just been born as their origins are actually related to bitcoins and the projects born to manipulate them. The history of NFTs is recent, and with many branches, it is still being written, and it is continuously expanding with a really huge turnover. The decisive year for the rise of the first NFTs is 2017, when Ethereum begins to increase its importance by announcing its own collection of Meme Pepe and then with the Cryptopunks project.

Non-fungible tokens today have branches in several areas, including:

● **Sports**. One of the first investors within the NFT world was Mark Cuban,owner of an NBA franchise, and since then, the world's top professional basketball league and several soccer clubs and many other sports haverealized the importance of NFTs. NBA Top Shot is designed for true fans and collectors and is one of the first and most important NFT projects whenit comes to sports. Owning in an unequivocal way an exclusive video of an action performed by your favorite player is not a small thing. Sorare, on the other hand, empowers you to play fantasy soccer, having the ownership of the purchased stickers and creating real teams. Sport with non-fungible- tokens opens to fans in a completely new and different way.

● **Fashion**. Digital fashion is today the vanguard of fashion, limited editions, and much more make possible unique fashion shows and collections and brings a high level of liquidity to a fast-growing sector. Digital objects, in the case of fashion, can be paired with NFTs, but that's just the first step. In the future, NFTs will make fashion.

- **Collectibles**. Collecting based on NFTs has its own backbone economy. Itopens up to digital media in a completely different way than before, comingto meet the generations of the future. Under the name of collecting, different visions are brought forward: the desire and pleasure of interacting and owning unique objects or the desire to invest, collectors from all over the world love to own works of art whose value, over time, can increase andgenerate capital.

- **Art**. Art has always generated a lot of interest and is fertile ground for investors. Now that NFTs have entered the market, there is no turning back. Collecting is no longer the preserve of a single privileged class, auction houses no longer hold a monopoly, and digital artists have found a way to profit from their creations. The NFT era is a new era or art.

- **Gaming**. One of the industries that first believed in non-fungible-tokens and received significant benefits from them is gaming. The market was ready; gamers have always been familiar with buying and selling, and exchanging digital assets. The problem was that until now, they were buying something they couldn't really claim ownership of. The non- fungible tokens purchased now are verifiable and authentic. They create value for the players themselves and also lead to new forms of collecting; inthis sector, NFTs are not just a trend, a fad but something that is already revolutionizing the market.

- **Real Estate**. The digital real estate sector provides a cost of production ofland that borders on zero. Its true value is really connected to its uniqueness, to the fact of owning an asset or, better, an original and unique token. Here the convergence between real and digital has its highest expression. It becomes a thin line of demarcation, almost impossible to see. In places like Decentraland, it is possible to have your own store, with digital assets linked to a clothing chain and much more. Several artists havecreated NFT villas and collections to visit as well as huge virtual events. Onthese marketplaces, the value of a property or a piece of land becomesmuch higher than the real one, and a digital property is sold in a second without any need of a middleman.

- **Music**. From Mike Shinoda of Linkin Park to Kings of Leon up to Grimes, Elon Musk's partner, many artists are betting on NFT in a reliable and evident way. The first great passage from physical to digital music has been a lost race for many entrepreneurial realities that don't seem to have any desire to let this further innovation escape.

Create an identity identifier. Digitizing documents of any kind while maintaining their uniqueness is a unique method of eliminating the possibility of fraud and creating a digital space where individual identity is recognized and protected.

These and many other undiscovered areas are the fertile ground where these tokens are exploding, generating a multi-million-dollar business. If the classic economy has always been based on the concept of scarcity to define the art, the network has undermined this concept. The web market is overabundant and disintermediated. For this, the NFTs are born to bring back the value of the assets of the market inside the Internet. With their own demonstrable uniqueness, NFTs are objects, works of art, music, and more that bring the concept of scarcity and perceived value of uniqueness into a world like the hyper-productive web.

There are many marketplaces where you can sell or produce your own tokens. Among the most popular and most used in different areas, there are Opensea, SuperRare, Nifty Gateway, NBA Top Shot, Sorare, and Rarible are just some of the most famous. Specifically, for Real Estate, everything revolves around platforms like Decentraland, Superworld, and The Sandbox. We are witnessing the convergence of real and digital. This is because digital real estate has a cost of land production practically zero, and its value is linked to perceived scarcity precisely because it is NFT.

Today creating a store, a house, or any digital asset that can be connected to Real Estate is possible and convenient. Thanks to smart contracts, it is, in fact, possible to acquire and establish ownership of different digital realities. Thanks to NFTs, it is possible to own a digital house in which to insert virtual works, always in ERC-20, or to proceed like the big brands, which open virtual stores where it is possible to buy tokens of everything displayed there. Virtual events within Decentraland, for example, can be much more profitable and require less effort than real ones. Because of this, many companies realize that having a virtual store allows for staggering sales. Overpricing is often questioned when in reality, the value of virtual land is potentially higher: a Decentraland store and storefront will enable you to reach many more people than the same store on a real street.

Demand and collective confidence in the value of the virtual real estate is growing, and the change is happening fast. Another advantage of digital real estate is based on the ability to transfer ownership of the token and what is inside it in a practical and fast way. This transferability is much quicker and less expensive, and most importantly, does not require intermediaries. Transactions on Ethereum platforms are based on a transparent, unalterable, immutable, and unchangeable consensus mechanism.

It is the first time that users worldwide can create NFTs that these can be immediately available in marketplaces. Here people can buy, trade, sell and auction NFTs. The significance of this property lies in the fact that we are moving from sales within closed marketplaces to the possibilities offered by a marketplace that has an open and free economy. The ease with which users can create and then trade NFTs around the world through the blockchain is impressive and can bring many changes to the real estate industry. Transferability allows NFTs to be sold at a higher price than the real thing:

> Digital property can be sold in minutes without the need for a broker.

> Registration is self-contained.

> The property needs no maintenance.

Moreover, thanks to the smart contracts that

regulate the transactions, each NFT provides a unique and non-falsifiable signature. The owners can then prove the provenance, making this type of purchase a more profitable and realistic investment. The virtual property built by contemporary artist KristaKim is called "Mars House" and is a property that sold for $500,000. Mars House has a design conceived by rounded lines and edges and furnished with fine glass furniture. Kim collaborated with musician Jeff Schroeder of Smashing Pumpkins, who composed the ambient soundtrack introducingthe virtual property.

The owner of this virtual home receives the unique file of the project that can be uploaded to three-dimensional worlds like Decentraland and experience its augmented reality. An artist like Kim believes that the NFT real estate market can parallel the real one. Also, the home's furniture canbe built in real-life replication by select Italian glass furniture manufacturers.

Real estate is notoriously slow to adopt new technologies. However, the very nature of real estate makes it ideal for blockchain applications: it is immobile and easily available to third parties with blockchain-based claims on it, such as collateral. The world of digital assets is expanding, and we are only now starting to see every part of daily life and business activities converted into a computer-readable format. Money is already digital; just think that only 8% of the world's currency materializes in the form of cash. Through blockchain, exchanges, transactions, and sales will begin to have fewer problems. Through the use of these digitized platforms, key stakeholders will see increased speed and lower transaction costs, alongwith an increase in available data. Transaction transparency, along with privacy protection, is essential when it comes to creating a healthy environment for buyers, sellers, and real estate agents.

NFT & REAL ESTATE: THAT'S AMAZING NEWS!

THE NEW FRONTIER OF VIRTUAL WORLDS

Many tangible items are now also coming to exist in NFT versions—everything from Nike shoes and NBA videos to crypto artworkand crypto kittens. Real estate is next. Virtual real estate represents the newest frontier of an already new market, and real estateinvestors from all over the world will not miss the opportunity to be amongthe pioneers of this new land. Wherever you are in the real world, you canlog into a virtual world based on the blockchain. Moreover, you can access this virtual world through avatars that can occupy, buy, and resell entire properties.

It's not just about games: the popularity of virtual worlds like Decentraland and Cryptovoxels is expanding. In February 2021, a lot on Axie Infinity sold for $1.5 million before total virtual land sales peaked at over $6million. This is a historical time and full of exciting opportunities for real estate. These metaverses are secure, and the smart contracts that handle transactions on the blockchain record and regulate every movement orproperty. Many people buy virtual homes to showcase their crypto artNFTs. They are basically art incubators hosting virtual galleries where they can have other avatars admire the properties they buy. The digital resources found in metaverses like Decentraland are part of a new kind of creative economy whose structure mirrors that of video games like Minecraft and Animal Crossing with the difference that in The Sandbox and Decentraland users can actually own the land they are building on.

Traditional practices have been turned upside down. The user can afford to do things that would not be possible in reality, such as interact with artwork. Virtual lands promise to transform and democratize the artistic experience, as well as the real experience. Anyone can enter a metaverse, acquire real property within it, and enjoy the rents on that property. Moreover, as the game becomes an opportunity, art enthusiasts have space to perform and continue expanding their digital horizons. It's a whole new world in whichto participate, socialize, invest, and earn.

UPLAND: AN ALTERNATIVE WORLD MADE OF LLAMAS

https://play.upland.me/

Upland, a globally distributed platform based in Silicon Valley and founded by entrepreneurs Dirk Lueth, Mani Honigstein, and Idan Zuckerman, all started in 2018 during a game of Monopoly. The research and development center is located in Ukraine, where collectibles featured in video games based on blockchain technology started to make headlines in 2018. The combination of Monopoly and collectibles sparked the idea of tokenizing the real world.

Upland is a metaverse where people can play, but they can also socialize and, most importantly, earn money. For this reason, the platform is designed to be easy, understandable to all, and fun. It offers a virtual, augmented world experience and an opportunity for anyone to make some pretty good money.

Monetization on Upland is similar to a game that allows you to buy and sell real estate based on an actual map. The game screen is a little different from Google Maps, where you can move on real streets and view real buildings. This is a metaverse, an alternative world where you can buy, sell, and rent properties. The map displays real streets with properties already bought or for sale and the resources that users have placed within them, turning them into profitable activities. By clicking on a single property, you can place your avatar in the area, find game clues, or see it live, but the real purposeof the game is to manage the purchased properties and resell them to the highest bidder. The game also includes rent collection and credits thataccumulate for each action taken, and these can be spent to obtain information about a home.

Upland's blockchain allows you to:
- have a secure record of every transaction;
- trade on a decentralized platform with no transaction fees; and,
- exchange tokens for traditional currencies.

In partnership with Tilia Pay, Upland launched the first virtual trading asset for NFT in fiat, still only in USD, becoming the first platform to exchange virtual properties for cash. Thus, the game became very serious.

MARS HOUSE

https://vimeo.com/416558553

Real estate, digital, and art meet dematerialization in the cosmic void under the roof of Mars House, the hyper-futuristic house designed by Krista Kim and sold exclusively on SuperRare, in Ntf, for 288 Ether, the second most valued cryptocurrency, for now, after Bitcoin. Is the future of real estate really here? Let's just say it's an exciting and profitable opportunity for the industry.

Returning for a moment with our feet on Earth and trying to understand, as mere mortals, what happened, we can rewrite the story as follows: the space-accented villa, virtually designed by the artist who founded the Techism Movement, was purchased by the collective "Art On Internet" on the revolutionary platform dedicated to the trading of digital works of art for a sum equaling $ 514,557.79 (about 431,000 euros).

The house is there but does not exist: it's all true. The paradox of the phantom purchase melts away as soon as you understand the potential of Nft.

Let's imagine for a moment the Ntf as if they were dematerialized bricks. Everything they realize is intangible but purchasable. There is no property address, but the owner can exist. "As a Techism artist - a movement that reconciles technological innovation with creative inspiration - I am challenging the power Nft as an artistic medium," said Krista Kim, theSouth Korean-born Canadian founder of the Techism Movement. "Mars House will live forever as Nft."

The house, which goes beyond traditional architectural design and involves the canonical approach of a work of art, is a concept born from an idea that emerged during the pandemic. Space knows no limitations. Like a virtual canvas, it is an empty place to be filled and bridged.

A small piece of history in the real estate market, the Mars House is the firsthome ever sold this way. As previously stated, when digital content is sold through Nft, it doesn't become visible only to its owner but remains available on the web. Therefore, to discover the Mars House, all you have to do is find it on Vimeo.

You will find yourself afore a clip of almost three and

a half minutes, with astrong digital zen atmosphere, the result of Kim's collaboration with Jeff Shroeder, guitarist of the Smashing Pumpkins and creator of the musical base.

However, art on the Internet will also offer the possibility to share the concept to a metaverse, a 3D immersive world, to live it through virtual reality. Located among the Martian heights, the dwelling is about as futuristic as you could dream it to be. But patience; if theoretically transferred to the real world, it would be challenging - if not impossible - to achieve. Whatprimarily strikes us, in fact, is the absence of load-bearing walls holding theroof — an unusual but necessary renunciation, given the artist's desire to "create a meditative environment on our screen, like a digital Zen garden." Therefore, it is easy to understand how instead of - internal and external – walls, there only are continuous and transparent glass windows. In brief, space appears to know no limits, thus promoting the expansion of theconsciousness of those who inhabit it.

The interiors

Another peculiarity is the presence of only two rooms inside the house: a spacious living area with a huge curved sofa and a large dining table that stands out, and a bedroom with a double bed. There is no bathroom nor kitchen. Even the furniture, modern and essential, also seems to be made of glass. "They can be made both in reality by Italian glass furniture craftsmen

- reads SuperRare - and visualized through the technology of MicroLED screens." But there could also be sufficient room for a corner dedicated to digital art: "Everyone should install in their home a led wall for Nft art," said Kim. "This is the future, and the Mars House shows the beauty of this possibility."

The swimming pool

Outside, find out the fantastic infinity pool with sun loungers and sofas for sipping a drink by the water. However, getting into a bathing suit would require Wim Hof's tolerance to the cold. Indeed, temperatures on the planetrange from as low as -140°C in winter to as high as -14°C in summer. What's nice, however, is the possibility of illuminating the entire area with different colors through the lamps located inside the apartment.

Solidarity aim

Beyond its artistic value, it is essential to underline the solidarity purpose ofthe initiative. Kim and Schroeder have decided to allocate most of the proceeds from the sale of the Mars House to their Continuum Foundation. This organization will support a world tour of sound and light art installations to heal and improve mental well-being. "We want to remind future generations that we are here to create a new and better world," they said.

FLYING IN COLORS

A REAL HOUSE BECOMES AN NFT

https://dulgeroffnft.com/

Shane Dulgeroff, a brilliant and innovative American real estate agent, had a revolutionary idea: to sell the house located at 221 Dryden Street in Thousand Oaks, California, as an NFT. Thus, he put the house up for auction on the OpenSea marketplace. The idea is to use a virtual, decentralized platform to sell a real, physical property. Shane Dulgeroff is an innovative specialist and investor in the luxury real estate industry. His goal is to intercept real estate investors and stay on top of the market and its trends. He intends to explore new territory in the real estate industry. Exciting videos on Dulgeroff's website accompany the entire transaction, introducing the home to potential buyers.

The home is complete with a garden and pool and features two bedrooms, a kitchen with state-of-the-art appliances, a bathroom, and wood floors. It is not the home that has been tokenized; rather, an NFT of crypto art named "Flying in Colors" is available on OpenSea. The designer of the NFT is established crypto artist Kii Arens, who has worked with the likes of Lady Gaga, The Rolling Stones, Dolly Parton, Radiohead, and many more. With her art Arens, expresses her idea of the concept of home: the animation represents a lunar, pop vision of home and is a true work of crypto art with a digitally replicated view of the San Gabriel Mountains.

Shane Dugleroff's idea is to bridge the gap between the real and the virtual by having both interpenetrate. On the site, there are also documents about the house and the guide to buying the NFT. This is a real estate deal absolutely worth testing now that the market is still a bit undefined in terms of taxes and regulations specific to a sale of this type. The NFT video of the house is tied to the real property of the house so much that it is not possible to split the two properties. Moreover, Dugleroff has simplified the process of accessing real estate by bringing it to the attention of younger people and expanding toward an entirely new audience: digital investors.

Dulgeroff's initiative encountered some issues that caused the deal to fall through. Among them, we find three crucial considerations:

1. Potential NFT buyers faced a hurdle due to the additional costs involved when purchasing an investment property versus a purely digital asset. Indeed, even though it is connected to an NFT, the purchase of any real property has significant legal and tax implications for the buyer.

2. The gap between the two investment worlds that Dulgeroff sought to bridge was much more significant than he expected. That's because, behind the offering, there has to be a buyer who equally understands cryptocurrency and NFTs and the real estate market and property management. This requirement made it much more difficult, at least for now, to find an audience for the investment. The end-user of NFTs is a precise target audience because some purchases are aimed at a life in the digital wallet, and then, within the blockchain. Therefore, as a house needs proper maintenance, it is an entirely different investment.

3. Limiting yourself to crypto buyers still means cutting off a substantial portion of the real estate market.

However, we are confident that his attempt is promising and allows those who want to experiment creating real opportunities in the field to take advantage of the strengths and weaknesses brought out by Dulgeroff, who is looking for the best strategies to make this new market a disruptive and profitable innovation.

REAL ESTATE: NOT ONLY LUXURY BUT ALSO AFFORDABILITY WITHIN EVERYONE'S REACH

The news circulating on the Internet about the great sales and investors' interest in the NFT world make it seem like a sort of golden mystique has been created around it. This is not entirely true.

The NFT world is open to everyone, and this initiative proves it. The non- fungible-token world is cloaked in a shiny aura of luxury and glitz, but this is only a partial view. NFTs open the door to unparalleled democratization in investing that is impossible anywhere else. It is by following this principle that blockchain platform Enjin and LABS Group have begun a collaboration that opens the door to low-cost, affordable real estate investments.

Fractioning high-yield properties such as luxury apartments, villas, andhotels in the form of tokens will allow small and micro-investors to enter a market hitherto precluded to them while also providing additional benefits that ultimately open to a new era in the real estate market. Transactions processed through Ethereum will allow both buyers and owners of largereal estate assets to cut down on the high costs of using third parties and eliminate the long waiting times due to national and supranational regulations.

The tokenization of small fractions of prime real estate will allow for alarge infusion of liquidity into the global real estate market, creating the largest asset class in the world with an estimated value of $228 trillion.

NFTs created through Enjin will be integrated into the LABS Group's platform, where only approved property owners will be able to coin their own NFTs. All of this will be protected by both the inherent properties of the blockchain and the LABS Security Exchange regulation.

With a price tag of only $100 per fraction of NFT, anyone will be able to invest in and hold ownership of a portion of a luxury resort, hotel rooms, and even entire buildings. Investors will be able to store and manage their real estate assets within Enjin's blockchain wallet and verify the ownership, origin, authenticity, and uniqueness of the digital NFT, which is a unique way of combining the real and the digital to create a democratic win-win system. Investors will be able to boast ownership of a portion of a luxury property by sharing dividends, while real estate developers will have the opportunity to create liquidity.

862 FENIMORE, NEW YORK: ART AND REAL ESTATE MEET THANKS TO NFTS

https://www.862fenimore.com/

The house listed as NFT on OpenSea on April 8, 2021 is not simply a home but a work of art created by the famous American architect Paul Rudolph, founder of the prestigious Saratosa School of Architecture and deus ex machina behind the construction of legendary buildings around the world. Rudolph worked on this project throughout the 1980s, planning additions and improvements that would make the buildinga truly timeless jewel.

Today, this rare historic building has been

remodeled under careful supervision to keep the original idea intact. Solar panels, ecological foam, and geothermal systems were added to make the house a zero-emission home while implementing all the amenities of 21st-century luxury. Thus, the home of the future is a 9,000-sq ft. historic building on 2.49 acres of land.

The innovation of the project is that with an auction base of 1 Ether and a reporting fee of 2%, it is possible to access the auction and win the NFT of this building of absolute prestige whose real price, as quoted by the Paul Rudolph Heritage Foundation and the Paul Rudolph Foundation, would be impossible for most people. In this case, tokenization enables an extraordinary opportunity because whoever wins the auction will own the NFT and the real property connected to it.

Whoever wins "The World's First Art as Architecture NFT," in addition to owning a unique piece, will also receive ownership of the physical house represented by the enclosed:

- Certificate of ownership of the physical residence
- Possession of all control systems connected to it

- All appliances and furniture in the home

In an unstoppable process, the blockchain and the world of non-fungible tokens are interacting with and interpenetrating physical reality thanks tothe possibilities of real estate. New investment possibilities that were previously impossible to imagine are now opening up and promising to change the world of the global real estate market.

NFT REAL ESTATE IN SAN FRANCISCO

Jered Kenna, founding entrepreneur and CEO of 20mission Co- living/20mission Cerveza, is auctioning off a rather substantial NFT:the rights to a 75-year lease in his 20Mission co-living space, paid in the form of an NFT. Whoever wins the auction will pay $1 a month and no utility fees for the co-living space in a 41-unit building in the Mission District, where tenants regularly pay up to $2,200 in monthly rent.

This innovative project will tokenize physical rather than virtual properties for the first time, thus revolutionizing the real estate industry as there is no direct precedent for an NFT lease. And in the wake of Dulgeroff, the real estate agent who tried to sell a property by associating it with a piece of crypto art in NFT, this initiative explores another direction, envisioning a long-term project. The famous Bitcoin house auctioning off the lease is located in the heart of the Silicon Valley startup community. In addition to the lease, the auction winners will receive an additional NFT that gives them the exclusive right to use the purchased space as a virtual asset.

Developed by Jered Kenna, Bitcoin exchange pioneer and founder of the first Bitcoin exchange in the United States, 20Mission is a cryptographic landmark of the very first Bitcoin house. It hosted the first San Francisco Bitcoin meetups, the first Bitcoin art show, and was also the site of the first documentary about the currency, *The Rise and Rise of Bitcoin,* released in 2014.

20Mission owns luxurious co-living spaces located in the heart of SanFrancisco and fully equipped for living with a built-in startup community aimed at fostering entrepreneurship. Together, these commercial spaces andindividual rooms represent a

41-room community geared towards art, technology, and entrepreneurship, and located in the center of the Mission District. For this reason, Kenna's is a potentially winning strategy as it aims to attract numerous investors and young people interested in projects like this one, who will become the tenants of the home and will not have to pay additional taxes for it.

Jered Kenna is striving to replicate the success that NFTs have encountered while selling virtual properties by introducing a completely new model that can disrupt the real estate market. It's a sizable bet worth monitoring. The building has intrinsic value for its historicity and influence. Still, it is considered a suitable investment property whose rental appears to be facilitated and made more fluid and convenient for everyone.

QBC ENGADINE SA: THE TOKEN BUSINESS

Qbc Engadine SA is a newborn, St. Moritz-based company with a very ambitious goal: to simplify the bureaucracy associated with the transfer of ownership of various digital assets. The business is linked to the Quantico Business Club, an exclusive group of entrepreneurs that offers its members assistance, know-how, and confidential networking to create new business opportunities. Already very active in the growth of SMEs, this reality is now introduced to NFT investments with Qbc Engadine SA.

Qbc Engadine was created to buy, sell, and manage real estate assets sold inthe form of cryptographic tokens. This company's first project will consist of distributing and making the building's property with six apartments saleable via blockchain. Leading the project will be the administrator, Gianluca Massimo Rosati, well known for his tax escapology techniques and ability to make transactions between company's fluid and secure.

Also, part of the project are strategic partners:

The Great Living Estate, an agency specializing in the search and renovation of prestige and luxury properties;

Luxochain, an agency active since 2017 in the production of NFTs that will lead the tokenization process;

Terrabitcoin Club, a club of large crypto investors.

The company was created to take advantage of the great ferment around NFTs and the legal benefits of transactions through cryptocurrency, which can count on a more streamlined, more accessible, transparent, and secure real estate sales system.

10 MILLION EUROS AVAILABLE FOR DIGITAL ASSETS

German stock exchange operator and security exchange platform Deutsche Börse, along with German bank Commerzbank, have invested in a new platform called 360X, which aims to create new markets for digital assets. For now, 360X focuses on supporting investments in art and real estate.

Thus, banks and credit institutions are taking over the virtual real estate and crypto art markets to support the trading of non-fungible NFT tokens. Carlo Kölzer, founder and CEO of 360X, said they selected art and real estate because, historically, both have proven to be illiquid markets. 360X's goal is to make many more things investable. And to do so, the German company has invested as much as 10 million euros for a roughly 50 percent stake in 360X, while Commerzbank owns a smaller share.

Kölzer and his colleagues had already worked together when founding 360T, an electronic foreign exchange platform, in Frankfurt, in 2000. Meanwhile, Deutsche Borse and Commerzbank experimented with blockchain technology in 2019. Now, with more experience and a vision axed on the future, they are ready to enter the NFT field. The real estate market is resilient and constantly changing, has been able to withstand disastrous inflections, and always supports good money circulation. The virtual real estate market appears leaner, faster, agile, able to allow incredible earning opportunities, and has a smoother and simplified management of national and international rules since the exchange of digital assets in blockchain follows the rules of smart contracts.

HOW MUCH CAN A VIRTUAL REAL ESTATE PROPERTY BE WORTH?

When we talk about NFT, we often talk about records. Well, even inthe field of virtual real estate, a record has been broken thanks toa game, Axie Infinity, a universe of tokenized digital animals in which players fight, care for, mate with, and exchange fantasy creatures called Axies. Again, this is a game to be taken seriously, and many have long understood this. The sensational purchase concerns as many as nine blocks of Genesis land for the sum of 888.25 ethe (although the currency in the game is called Moon), which is equivalent to $1.5 million. This transaction represents the largest ever NFT transaction of Genesis land, which is highly valued property due to being rare and better placed in the game.

The "lands" on Axie Infinity allow you to generate

infinite resources. Owning land in this metaverse is already very rare, as all lots have now been sold. Thus, the possibilities of gain for those who are active on the platform multiply exponentially. If you own a lot, you can build structures on it, create potions or other resources that can be used in the game, and acquire a decisive role by placing features such as rivers or roads in your lots.

In this game, the sale of virtual lands is a real event offered in the form of an auction, and every single quadrant of land contains trunks and treasure chests that enrich the user's experience. Located in the center of the map, Genesis land is scarce, as it is limited to 220 plots. Activity in the virtual lands, incentivized by a system that rewards users with fantastic new experiences, involves more showing off than playing. This game allows you to make virtual real estate purchases and acquires value based on the players' consent. The value of virtual appreciation is increasing by leaps and bounds, and the real estate industry should take advantage of this digital renaissance. Axie Infinity also plans to launch an interactive system called "Project K" that will allow players to explore, decorate, fight, and collect resources on their virtual land. In addition, the platform is constantly being revamped, even allowing players to bypass the considerable gas fees thanks to the Ronin sidechain developed by Sky Mavis and installable as a Chrome extension. Moreover, there are many other exciting projects in sight, such asthe development of Android and Apple apps.

NFT & REAL ESTATE DISRUPTIVE PROJECTS

AXIE INFINITY

https://axieinfinity.com/

This game involves users taking care of small pets, very similar to Pokémon. These pets are designed to socialize, fight, accumulate points, get improvements, and reproduce. Another interesting thing you can do on Axie Infinity is buy land and own your own home. Axie Infinity animals move on the blockchain and are made according to ERC-20 tokens—i.e., AXS, the platform's native token.

In games based on the Ethereum network, you can successfully earn cryptocurrencies or contribute to the ecosystem by creating value. You can develop these properties over time and upgrade them. This world waslaunched in 2018, and all game actions have always been registered on the Ethereum network. Each tiny animal has its own characteristics and abilitiesin combat, and each of them has been able to gather communities around them that are enriched daily with new players. Although it is taken for granted today, at the time of its arrival, Axie Infinity's ease of use and infinite possibilities revolutionized game play. Today, it is constantly evolving while remaining reliably based its original features.

In 2020, the game became part of Binance Launchpad, which ensures the development of the entire game economy and acts as its support by accessing a centralized exchange platform. Binance Launchpad is a feature of the platform that allows tokens to be launched on Binance. Startups that want to develop their own tokens here can do so by leveraging the Binance brand to gain notoriety. At the same time, investors are assured that the platform has done extensive research to ensure the reliability of the company.

Due to the high investor traffic, the platform has created a lottery to keepthe whole service fair. To participate in the lottery, you need lottery tickets. The tickets are given out according to how many BNB are present in the wallet. If you are chosen during the lottery, you have the opportunity to acquire tokens and tokens of the start-ups. In the marketplace on the site, you can see the volume that the game has generated. In the marketplace, you can buy characters and lands divided into different classes. Pairing, reproducing, and making the game characters evolve means having a real possibility of increasing the value of and then selling your tokens. That's why it's crucial to understand how the game works.

The collectible creatures have different powers and abilities to be acquired and enhanced. Their fight takes place within the land, which is calledprecisely "land." The combat takes place on turns, and the power of these tiny monsters resides in the various parts of their bodies, such as the mouth, the tail, the back, and the horns. It is these characteristics that determine the statistics and abilities that you can use. Axie organizes events and tournaments to give out prizes. The contests celebrate essential partnershipssuch as the one formed in 2020 with Ubisoft Entrepreneur Labs. The landscape plays a significant role in the game. Lunacia, as the world ofAxie Infinity is called, is composed of four types of land:

Savannah Forest
Artic Mystic

There are also special lands, such as Genesis land and Luna's land. Each land contains placed items and resources, and each land type grants skill boosts to little Axie. Lunacia consists of tokenized land appreciations that can be sold, bought, and rented by players. The owner can customize the land to house stores, markets, or crucial points in the game within theirland, such as dungeon entrances. The possibilities are truly endless. For instance, they can host structures and expand them over time or generate new resources that can be used, sold, and traded. As of today, land lots are finite. The only way to get new land is to make in-game purchases. The real estate sector cannot fail to take advantage of this historic moment: the land of Axie Infinity has a monetary, social, entertainment, and economic value not to be underestimated.

CRYPTOVOXELS

https://www.cryptovoxels.com/

In 2018, Nolan Consulting, an independent game developer based in Wellington, New Zealand, created Cryptovoxels. Initially a project to build a simple metaverse, the author saw its possible expansion via the Ethereum blockchain using a standard ERC721 token. Cryptovoxels is a Minecraft-style game but represents much more for real estate investors and users as it enables:

● The e-commerce of land, property, and more. Cryptovoxels allows users to truly own their items and the digital assets put in place. There, you can buy and sell lands, objects, artwork, and much more

● A wholly social world. It creates a space for sharing and socializing.

- Creative space and a video game. Cryptovoxels is a world created by users and editable by them. You can create stores, pubs where you can play, recording studios, art galleries, and anything else you can imagine.

The game's interface is very intuitive, which seriously expands its investment possibilities since it looks like a user-friendly virtual reality platform. Indeed, once users have connected their metamask wallet to the game, they will have an avatar, to which they can give a name and buy wearable devices. Once done and after buying land, they will be able tostart building whatever they want and wander freely around the city, buying and visiting places like in the real world. Although at this time, Cryptovoxels is mainly used as a base for virtual galleries of NFT and virtual conferences in augmented reality, the possibilities for economic expansion are numerous, hence why the lands in Origin City are all soldout.

The developers have thus announced the opening of Proxima Tower Island, a tower island connected to

Origin City by a bridge, where it will be possible to buy an apartment rather than land. The 80 apartments are for sale at $200 each, a much lower price tag than land in Origin City. They are being targeted by real estate investors who have understood the potential of a booming world, where you can buy and sell without the restrictions of international laws. Nolan has created a sandbox on the island, where you can now build your own objects without owning a parcel.

Cryptovoxels is a world in full expansion. A point of connection between investors, artists, auction houses, brands, and companies looking for a place of lasting interactions with the public, now that virtual reality for users is closer than ever to the real world. Investing in land in virtual worlds, like this one, means opening the doors to the digital innovation of the metaverse, which is increasingly conquering future generations and positioning oneself at the forefront of a lively and decidedly remunerative market.

DECENTRALAND

https://decentraland.org/

Decentraland (MANA) presents a virtual-reality platform based on the Ethereum blockchain. With it, users can build applications and content while generating revenue.

It is the first trustworthy decentralized virtual platform that sets apart from the crowd, set up on the blockchain, and is possessed by its users.

Who developed the platform?

The Decentraland team has expertise in cryptocurrency, one among many of their projects being the invention of Bitcore (BTX). The leader of the project, Ari Meilich, partnered with technical manager Esteban Ordano.

The advisory board includes:

- ☐ Xiaolai Li (the founder of INBlockchain);
- ☐ Jake Brukhman (the creator of CoinFund);
- ☐ Luis Cuende (the head of the Aragon project);
- ☐ Diego Doval (the former CTO of Ning).

Additionally, Decentraland operates with two other cryptocurrencies, Aragon and District0x.

Currently, there are literally no limits with Decentraland. Using this platform, anything can be created and explored. Users can buy land using the Ethereum blockchain that indisputably confirms ownership.

As a user, you are free to create whatever you desire. Some of the options proposed by the Decentraland team cover live music shows, casinos, shopping, commercial activities, visits to underwater resorts, and test drivesfor cars.

All of this takes place in a virtual world with a 360-degree view that can engage users through the web browser or by using a VR visor.

What sets Decentraland apart from other VR platforms?

The most meaningful difference between Decentraland (MANA) and existing VR platforms is its ownership.

The team following the project thinks that public virtual worlds should be managed and governed with open standards. In other words, no central organization should force its will.

In addition to being possessed by users, Decentraland enables them to control the plot of land they own entirely. Also, the owners can derive income from the value generated by other users.

Besides, Decentraland is utterly distinctive from systems where the central organization, which runs the platform, takes a percentage of every transaction. Without a point of centralization, no group can decide on commissions or fees to be paid. All of this is possible, as mentioned above, through Decentraland's (MANA) use of blockchain technology, which uniquely certifies ownership of a parcel.

How to purchase land?

Buying land is as easy as using MANA, Decentraland's token. Land tiles measure 10 square meters, and there are no limits on vertical buildings; the only constraints are on the base of the constructions.

Although, it is relevant to note that Decentraland's

arth tiles are sparse. They were especially and purposely designed to increase demand for it and improve the overall user experience and ability to discover its contents.

If the lands were huge, they would never be explored and would also cost very little. Registration for the Terraform Event closed on December 15, 2017.

What is the goal of the MANA token?

MANA is used to purchase lands, either directly from Decentraland or from other users as lands are transferable, and to buy digital goods and services found in the virtual world. The utility of MANA will grow as Decentraland's lands are developed on the Ethereum blockchain. You can buy MANA tokens on leading exchanges. A complete list is available on CoinMarketCap, and they can be stored in an Ethereum wallet.

What are the projects for the future?

The Decentraland project was launched in June 2015, in what they call theStone Age, when the earth was modeled in the form of a simple grid andpixels were allocated to users by a Proof of Work algorithm. In March2017, the project set foot in the Bronze Age, and a 3D view was added. Those who purchased MANA, the ERC20 token, were able to get plots ofland and then interact with other holders of the same cryptocurrency. Later,the Iron Age added multiplayer support, along with a live chat and avatars. The last period, the Silicon Age, has opened the world to full VR support.

In March 2018, the group launched the Decentraland Marketplace, a decentralized marketplace, as the name suggests, where you can purchase and sell land belonging to other users.

ETHERLAND

https://etherland.world/

When buying or selling a property, it is essential to have a document that serves as a record and displays all the information that can be found about that land or property. This document, called the cadaster, is used in many countries according to the guidelines established by Napoleon in 1807. However, in other nations, it is not common practice. There, the sale is instead publicly displayed so that it can be verified. This process is an example of decentralization through which it remains challenging to trace sales that are often difficult to prove. This is where Etherland comes in.

Through a worldwide registry known as Estatepedia, Etherland connects real estate units from across the world, allowing people to create, own, and maintain information in an efficiently and transparently. Etherland will empower people to gain control over legal documents, images, terrains data, solar exposure, and more while creating NFTs aimed at developing an entire ecosystem that is a metaverse parallel to that of the Earth. The Etherland platform is an aggregate of interoperable technologies that connect users' digital data with the physical world. It is essentially a decentralized repository that provides free access to information anytime, and from anywhere in the world, for an almost infinite period.

Etherland was created as a solution to the lack of information or its malicious management by the owners. In this way, Etherland binds the owner to their property's information by providing a complete history comprising updates, information, and ownership changes.

The created token is called LAND ID, and on the metaverse, you will have complete control over the property data stored in it, which also be modified. Etherland is the first global Estatepedia running on the Ethereum blockchain that will change the management of land ownership identification, possibly by converting or integrating paper documents into ERC721 tokens and unique IPFS data. The actual owner of the property you wish to digitize can thus have a Verified LAND ID, provided you have sufficient legal information. Since blockchain technology is accepted as legal proof in several countries worldwide, you can get double proof of ownership.

A LAND ID can contain the following information:

- Country
- Type of land
- Type of infrastructure
- City

- Number of issues

For instance, Big Ben has the following identification: GB.LML1, Britain, Landmark, Monument, London, and 1. So far, mainly world monuments have been mined on Etherland.

In addition, the platform has announced the arrival of the application thanksto which users from all over the world will be able to own rare NFTs by capturing them via their smartphones, as a real treasure hunt during which players will be able to secure ownership of these NFTs. Some of those are free and hidden on the map.

MERIDIO

https://www.cofi.tech/

Meridio is another platform based on Ethereum blockchain technology and is dedicated to the fractional ownership of the real estate. It represents one of the thrilling opportunities to create private investments, offering the possibility to reduce and potentially eliminate the various problems of accessibility to real estate investments. The basic idea is that you can own part of a real estate property, forexample, a building with offices inside or a store in a trendy neighborhood. With Meridio, you can own a part of that building and do so more easily, a method that also allows investors to resell the fractional property and get instant liquidity quickly. The blockchain substantially reduces the cost of a transaction. It will enable you to finance the property transparently because this asset offers all the metadata essential to choose the best property based on your expectations.

Therefore, Meridio aims to provide transparency and clear information to make the real estate market more liquid, accessible, and efficient for different levels of investors, from individuals to large companies. Its founders, Mo Shaikh and Corbin Page, started exploring the various possibilities that blockchain could offer until they decided to put their ideas together and found Meridio. As far as investors are concerned, Meridio offers several advantages:

1. It doesn't require a minimum investment or seed capital;
2. It reduces transaction costs, which occur in peer-to-peer and direct;
3. It develops the liquidity of the portfolio by allowing shares or bondsto be relocated.

On the other hand, once ownership of a property on Meridio has been obtained, it is possible to:

1. Unlock additional capital;
2. Streamline transaction processes through smart contracts;
3. Analyze asset-specific data in real-time.

The blockchain industry is moving beyond speculation. With platforms like Meridio, it is entering the era of utility and getting a substantial idea of real estate's future. Meridio runs on ConsenSys, the platform founded by Joseph Lubin, in New York, that operates on the Ethereum blockchain. The integrated stable coin is Maker's DAI. Using a stable coin allows for the benefits of having smart contracts included in trustless transactions and virtually instant timing while avoiding the volatility of cryptocurrency.

In addition, users can purchase or exchange tokens in the app directly with DAI in a direct, trustless exchange between tokens and DAI, meaning the transaction can happen without an escrow service and without being subject to unspecified price volatility.

Meridio has integrated the Airswap widget into users' wallets so they can quickly convert any Ether they hold in Metamask to DAI. The wallet page provides each user with the DAI and ETH balance of their linked wallet so that they can quickly see their current position and convert currenciesaccordingly.

OVR

https://www.ovr.ai/

It is safe to say that as of 2020, the real estate market has seen a new boom in the virtual land sector. It has indeed seen a substantial increase in supply and demand. Perhaps also due to the pandemic, there has been

a greater attraction to virtual lands, which many investors have purchased. Virtual lands are in great demand for various reasons, the first of all being profit:

● On virtual lands, it is possible to place structures and create real virtual galleries containing crypto artworks.

● You can rent and sell.

● You may host crypto games. A booming universe of possibilities is feasible thanks to blockchain technology.

● You get to decide in full autonomy the type of experience that the user can live.

In this context, OVR, an open-source augmented

reality platform built on the Ethereum blockchain that provides users with virtual experiences inside a virtual land called OVRLand, is positioned in full relief. OVR recently became known because of a disruptive piece of news: until April 30, 2021, it was possible to purchase the Eiffel Tower in the form of NFT tokens with an auction base of $7,400. Overall, OVR has sold over 200,000 NFTs from its OVRLand in the four months since its launch, and on April 27, in collaboration with artists Giovanni Motta, Marco Biscardi, and Rok Bogataj, it opened an art gallery that reached 7,000 views in just a few hours.

The new real-time digital experience is made possible on your smartphone or camera. The OVR app is available on both Android and Apple stores. It allows users with a mobile device or smart glass to enjoy personalized, interactive augmented reality experiences in the real world. It can be

defined as a new standard in augmented reality, where geographic experiences are based on the user's location.

With OVR's augmented reality, everything is becoming possible, even partying together. Each user has their own 3D avatar, which can interact with other users' avatars and participate in live performances. These experiences are available in augmented reality with more original scenery, lighting effects, and animals of all kinds, all within your own home, which you can completely transform. OVR is the brainchild of Italian CEO Davide Cuttini. OVR has operational headquarters in Italy, precisely in Udine, while the platform sees its international headquarters in Estonia.

The OVR ecosystem is supported by a grid of hexagons covering theEarth's entire surface, called "Over the Planet." The hexagons, called OVRLands, have a specific geographic location and a standard size of 300 square meters. ERC-721 tokens allow for decentralized ownership of the resource and experiences within it. OVRLand can be divided into multiple hexagons that allow for more precise localization within the possession. This means that owners who have invested in a land will be able to decidein full autonomy what kind of experience the user may have once inside. These OVRLands can be traded freely between users in a decentralized way through the OVR Owner marketplace. Thus, as on any decentralized platform, the community has complete control over OVRLands and OVR Experiences.

Economic incentives, development, and growth are all possible for Land asset owners in OVRs, precisely because of the blockchain technology, which makes the scarce and unique asset controllable by the owner alone. To purchase OVRLands, one must own a metamask wallet. The land can bechosen at will by bidding to purchase it. The programming is user-friendly and potentially open to any activity. For example, an artist can buy a gallery in which to display and sell his crypto artworks or charge an entrance fee, rent, and much more.

You can also stake the OVR token in three different ways:

- A 5% annual interest with no strings attached to the amount of tokens.

- A 15% interest for a 10-month block.

- Rewards for solving blockchain nodes.

The possible investments on OVR are infinite. It is a fertile ground for exciting ideas and projects in uninterrupted growth and with a considerable opportunity to make a profit. A project certainly to be monitored and in which it is worth considering investing.

REPUBLIC REALM

https://www.republicrealm.com/

Republic Realm is an online investment platform that saw the light in 2016 thanks to the collaboration of the two founders, Ken Nguyen and Bryant Mint. Headquartered in New York and San Francisco, the company's office network expands to Moscow, Shanghai, and Tel Aviv. The platform has investors from all over the world, among which are some of the giants in the industry, such as:

- Binance;
- Passport Capital;
- Tribe Capital;
- Zhen Fund;
- Venture Capital, and private investors.

What Republic Realm offers is a unique investment opportunity in real estate. Through the platform, investors will be equipped to interact on all metaverse existing today, and will then be able to:

☐ Acquire.

☐ Manage.

☐ Develop. Applying the principles of real-world development, the platform aims to create memorable spaces that are points of attraction and focus on the various metaverses that increase interaction possibilities.

☐ Buy and sell virtual land.

Where? On metaverses ranging from Decentraland to Axie Infinity via The Sandbox, Cryptovoxels, Somnium Space, and many more. Creating, publishing, and monetizing through NFTs will then be possible on multiple parallel digital universes through a single decentralized platform. This investment fund focuses on exclusivity, and thus, limits access to only 99 accredited investors and by invitation only.

Republic Realm's focal point is to create the intersection between the technological possibilities of virtual reality and blockchain. Being an investment ground with no real boundaries, that is extraordinarily malleable and will allow brands, companies, and investors from all over the world to seize a unique opportunity, the most avant-garde brands find in the metaverse the possibility to stimulate a whole new customer engagement. Musicians and crypto artists, gaming, lifestyle, and hospitality companies, as well as fashion and consumer brands are just some of the main targets that can invest in this platform.

After seeing what the investment opportunities are and the doors they open, we need to understand how to access them. As mentioned above, you can only enter this platform only by invitation. To try to be invited into this fund, you will need to fill out the information form available on the website, answer some concrete questions that will take into account your accreditations as an investor, the maximum capital you intend to invest, and a brief presentation of your project. After completing this process, the Republic Realm team will consider your application, and you will then receive feedback via email.

SOMNIUM SPACE

https://somniumspace.com/

Somnium Space is an open-source blockchain-based VR world within which you can tokenize your own custom VR avatars. This virtual world is characterized by a social one.

Within this world, you can, in fact:

Play and relax with many games; Socialize with other avatars;

Visit places and live virtual experiences; Rent or buy apartments, houses, or lands;

Have fun going to the movies, on rides, at the zoo, and much more.

No only a blockchain-based virtual game, Somnium Space is the world's first virtual world with equity crowdfunding. It is a new and unique game shaped by players who can meet, socialize, participate in events together, and monetize. Somnium Space's CEO and founder, Artur Sychov, worked for years as an investment trader before becoming a serial entrepreneur and has always firmly believed in the future of virtual worlds to develop human interaction.

So, in 2007, along with his able-bodied team, Sychov created a platform that aims to allow users to explore the virtual world. Through this decentralized blockchain platform, users can model augmented reality to choose to buy or sell land, participate in events, or organize them. SomniumSpace is a fully interconnected world accessible from any device, even in 2D.

However, the ownership of the virtual land is always at the base of the economy of virtual reality. Within your own land, it is, in fact, possible todo anything, and the game allows you to buy three types of lands:

1. A small parcel, which is equivalent to 10 meters in vertical andhorizontal limits;
2. A medium parcel that is 25 meters high and wide;
3. A large parcel that is 50 meters in upper development as well.

Each terrain can be increased, and additional resources can be purchased directly from the store. The customization possibilities are unlimited, and after building on your land, you can sell the result and monetize it if you wish to. On The Builder, the software that allows you to create on the properties, the only limit is your imagination. On the one hand, the blockchain enables the ownership of lands and assets, but on the other hand, it is possible to adjust one's layout configuration, record information regarding one's avatar, build anything the user wants, program one's experience, and monetize through it.

Somnium Space is an entirely immersive world in which the weather changes daily; if it's sunny, the buildings created by the users cast their shadows on the environment. All of this serves to awaken the body's senses and fuel the bond between the avatars. Users can actually own the land, just like in the real world. Using blockchain as its backbone, Somnium Space enables users to purchase plots of land, on which they can build whatever they want. And just like in real life, downtown land is more expensive because of its inherent appeal. In addition, the team developed a fullyfunctioning world loaded with events, encounters, and places to explore. People can enjoy live concerts, educational conferences, and sports competitions, or just sit in the park and watch the birds fly by. The virtual currency within this world is called Cube. Any NFT can be used within the platform and placed in the gallery, for example, thus allowing anyone to monetize their creations instantly. Somnium Space is one of those platforms that have allowed the virtual real estate sector to make that quantum leap and enter rightfully among the first choices of investors and entrepreneurs from around the world.

SUPERWORLD

https://www.superworldapp.com/

The platform, launched in 2017, was founded by Hrish Lotlikar and Max Woon, and uses the ERC-721 standard. Users who purchase land on SuperWorld own a non-fungible token with multiple monetization possibilities, including the opportunities to:

- ☐ Create virtual games.
- ☐ Open stores and e-commerce.
- ☐ Sell land.
- ☐ Create an augmented reality meeting place.
- ☐ Create exhibitions of artwork.

All the investment possibilities on a real plot of land seem potentially replicable on a digital plot of land in this metaverse. Properties not yet purchased on the platform have a base price of 0.1 ETH. They can be accessed by logging into SuperWorld and creating a wallet such as Metamask, Portis, or Fortmatic, and uploading Ethereum currency to it.

SuperWorld is one of the most notable metaverses within the NFT world and one of the most desirable for investors in digital real estate, with 64.8 billion virtual land parcels geographically mapped to the Earth. The entire globe has been mapped on the platform and is divided into 100 x 100 m polygonal real estate plots and put up for sale.

Today, a single stretch of Manhattan's High Line sells for over 333 ETH. The platform allows its users to own a unique piece of planet Earth and customize it according to their preferences, from augmented reality to 3D animations to audio, video, and text installations. This augmented reality will be visible not only by visiting SuperWorld but also by all those who, owning the specific app, will frame a particular place with their cellphones' cameras or VR glasses. In addition to the land, the platform offers endless opportunities to earn money through various initiatives, such as:

• NFT Saloon. There, NFT creators of all kinds can showcase and sell their creations: video games, crypto art, collectibles, music, and any other possible combination.

• Artist Resident. The goal is the creation of a living artistic community. That is why there is a list of resident artists, the best NFT artists owning properties, and land on the platform.

• SuperWorld Star Chamber. This is a virtual gallery where the platform showcases some of the most admired and appreciated non-fungible-token creators.

Investors and advisers include DraperGorenHolm, SOSV, CapitalFactory, Stephen Wolfram (creator of Mathematica and Wolfram Alpha), Bob Metcalfe (inventor of Ethernet and Metcalfe's Law), Richard Ling (founder of Rembrandt Ventures), Bob Fabbio (CEO of Tivoli), Robert Scoble (author, futurist), Mariana Danilovic, (founder of Infiom and Hollywood Portfolio), Phil Rowley (head of futures at Omnicom Group), Nitin Gaur (head of digital assets at IBM), Tobias Ratschiller (CEO of

CryptoCoinNews), Chris Thomas (head of digital assets at Swissquote Bank), William Burns (a pioneer of the metaverse), Brian Thorp (CEO of Wealthtender), and Joseph Chan (managing partner of Guardian Property Advisors).

THE SANDBOX

https://www.sandbox.game/en/

The Sandbox is the digital land buying and selling game on the blockchain, a set of products and services to create, manage, and enjoy various adventures and experiences.

What happens when blockchain, gaming, and real estate come together? Several experiments have been conducted over the years, but little has been discussed, and nothing has reached the broad public yet. However, this timearound, that could change: with the NFT craze filling the pages of the newspapers and business blogs, a project — more than three years indevelopment — is about to come within everyone's reach.

The Sandbox is a game about blockchain. It is its simplest definition, but it also is the one that makes less justice to the complexity of this project, which could impact the virtual real estate industry. Nowadays, The Sandbox is reaching its peak of notoriety and success. The platform is a set of products and services to create, manage, and enjoy experiences and adventures using the blockchain as a permanent ledger to give value and uniqueness to creation.

It's difficult to describe everything that can be done on The Sandbox. A few months ago, after a three-year development, the platform offered its first product, a map composed of 166,464 digital land plots which has been sold on multiple occasions. Now, the map is 45% complete, but there already are interesting economic dynamics that make one piece of land more meaningful than another. In general, the value of all the lots is increasing every day because the map has been fixed: when the lots to buy are finished, you can do nothing but rent them or use them for playing, among other things. Lots have been put up for sale directly on the website or are available for investment through an auction system on Opensea, one of the best-known NFT exchange platforms.

For example, in February alone, more than $2.8 million in lots were sold, and a single piece of land was auctioned for about $300,000. Those who purchase at such high prices do so for a single reason: some lots have strategic importance on the map. Some of the most influential buyers, in fact, are fundamental entities both in and outside of the crypto world. For instance, the video game and console manufacturer Atari bought lots for as much as $2 million. Meanwhile, Coinmarketcap (a data aggregator on all crypto) and Binance (the biggest exchange marketplace for crypto volumes in the world) both bought many lots, and this shows: it's all written on the blockchain.

Owning a lot close to a major brand means being capable to offer that lot to third-party customers by telling them about the proximity to products and services that everyone uses, precisely like when a real estate agent tries to convince someone to buy an apartment in downtown Rome rather than in the suburbs or in a small town many miles away. In both cases, proximity toservices (whether physical or digital) makes a difference. Indeed, because lots are not just pieces of land, like in Monopoly or the real world, you can build on them and construct a building with facilities and scenes that are suitable for one experience or another. For instance, Atari could create a colossal game with all the lots they got. At the same time, a developer could build a conference room to rent to communities and businesses that want to host events in distinctive scenarios.

On the one hand, there are the users of the world, and on the other hand, there are the creators. The latter, through a software package provided by The Sandbox, can both create games (with Game Maker) and design objects and characters (with VoxEdit), which they can then resell on the trading platform, available in beta version since March 30. In both circumstances, creators are digital artisans providing the elements or experiences that make The Sandbox a metaverse in its own right.

During this time of significant growth, the platform team has put together several initiatives to fund creators' work. At the launch of the beta platform, 46 artists had produced 112 creations, which can be added to their lands. Everything created is not owned by The Sandbox, but credited directly to the creator and recorded on the blockchain, thus allowing them to retain copyright.

The Sandbox is a reasonable example of the complexity that an application on the blockchain can achieve and how decentralization can be leveraged toredistribute wealth. The application is accessible via the Ethereum blockchain, which has been the star of a noteworthy increase in transaction volume over the past six months, leading to increased fees per transaction.

CRYPTO DUKEDOM

To know us a little more

We believe in the crypto world.

Our goal is to make it accessible to all people. For us, this is the future.

Or rather, the future that is already becoming present. There are new fantastic worlds, full of opportunities. There are difficulties, problems to be solved.

As in all things, we know it.

Thousands of people are working to solve them and constantly create newpossibilities. Even now.

We do our part by investing, sharing, and creating value for those like us who have approached all this inspired.

Thank you so much for choosing us!

Your satisfaction matters to us!

Did you like this book? Did you find it interesting and helpful? Is there anything you care about that we didn't cover?

We are always looking for ways to improve.

The topic is evolving so fast that we are committed to periodically improving our content.

Feel free to contact us at cryptodukedom@gmail.com

You trusted us. Your opinion is valuable to us.

And kindly leave us a review. It makes the difference.

We wish you the best. Crypto Dukedom.

Environmental awareness is important to us.

This book is printed-on-demand to reduce excess production. The ink is chlorine-free, and the acid-free interior paper stock is provided by a supplier certified by the Forest Stewardship Council.

We chose to print in black and white on cream-colored paper made with 30% post-consumer recycled material.

We choose minimalism and try to select the essential.

We believe you appreciate and share our choices.

We trust that you, together with us, will continue to revise your dailypractices to make sure we are doing our part to protect the environment.

CPSIA information can be obtained
at www.ICGtesting.com
Printed in the USA
LVHW021928260422
717236LV00009B/408